Symphony No. 2
in D Major, Op. 73

Johannes Brahms

DOVER PUBLICATIONS, INC.
Mineola, New York

Bibliographical Note

This Dover edition, first published in 1999, is a republication of music from "Symphonien für Orchester," edited by Hans Gál, from *Johannes Brahms, Sämtliche Werke / Ausgabe der Gesellschaft der Musikfreunde in Wien,* originally published by Breitkopf & Härtel, Leipzig, n.d.

International Standard Book Number: 0–486–40637-7

Manufactured in the United States of America
Dover Publications, Inc., 31 East 2nd Street, Mineola, N.Y. 11501

INSTRUMENTATION

2 Flutes [Flöten, Fl.]
2 Oboes [Oboen, Ob.]
2 Clarinets in A [Klarinetten, Klar.]
2 Bassoons [Fagotte, Fag.]

4 Horns in C, D, E, G, B ("H") [Hörner, Hr.]
2 Trumpets in D, B ("H") [Trompeten, Trpt.]
3 Trombones [Posaunen, Pos.]
and [und, u.]
Bass Tuba [Baßtub, Btb.]

Timpani [Pauken, Pk.]

Violins 1, 2 [Violine, Viol.]
Violas [Bratsche, Br.]
Cellos [Violoncell, Vcl.]
Basses [Kontrabaß, K.-B.]

CONTENTS

Symphony No. 2
in D Major, Op. 73
(1877)

Symphony No. 2

in D Major, Op. 73

I.

II.

III.

Allegretto grazioso (Quasi Andantino)

2 Flöten
2 Oboen
Klarinetten in A
2 Fagotte
1. Horn in G
u. 4. Horn in C
1. Violine
2. Violine
Bratsche
Violoncell
Kontrabaß

Allegretto grazioso (Quasi Andantino)

Presto ma non assai ($\s>

 = \>

$)

Presto ma non assai ($\>

 = \>

$)

94

sempre p

sempre p

sempre p

pp

pp

pp

pizz

107 **Tempo primo.**

dolce

dolce

dolce

dolce

C

f

f

mf

p

p

p

p

arco

p

mp

mp

mp

mp

mp

Tempo primo.

C

126 **Presto ma non assai**

Presto ma non assai

IV.

49

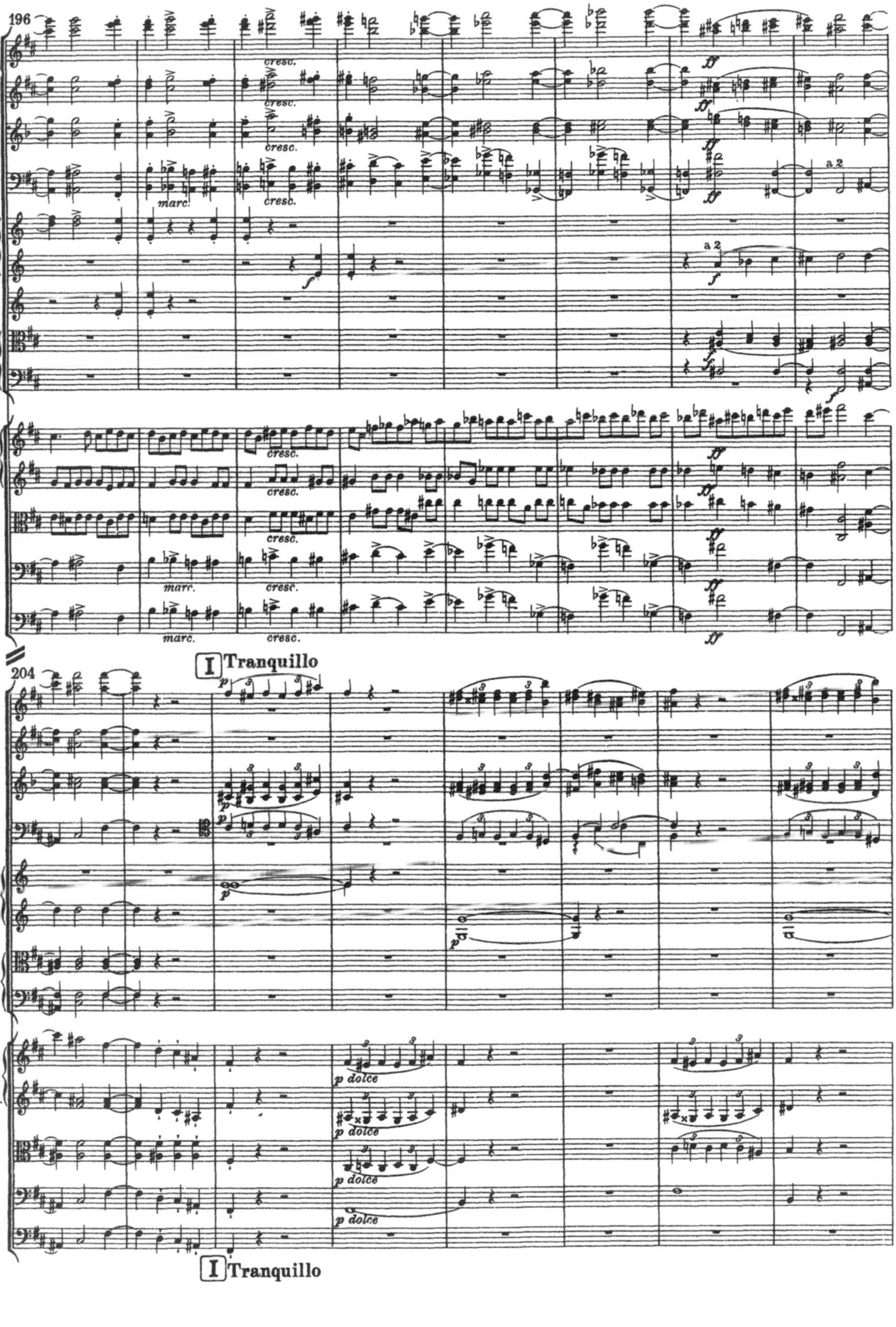
196
cresc.
marc.
ff
a 2
f
204
I Tranquillo
p
p dolce
I Tranquillo

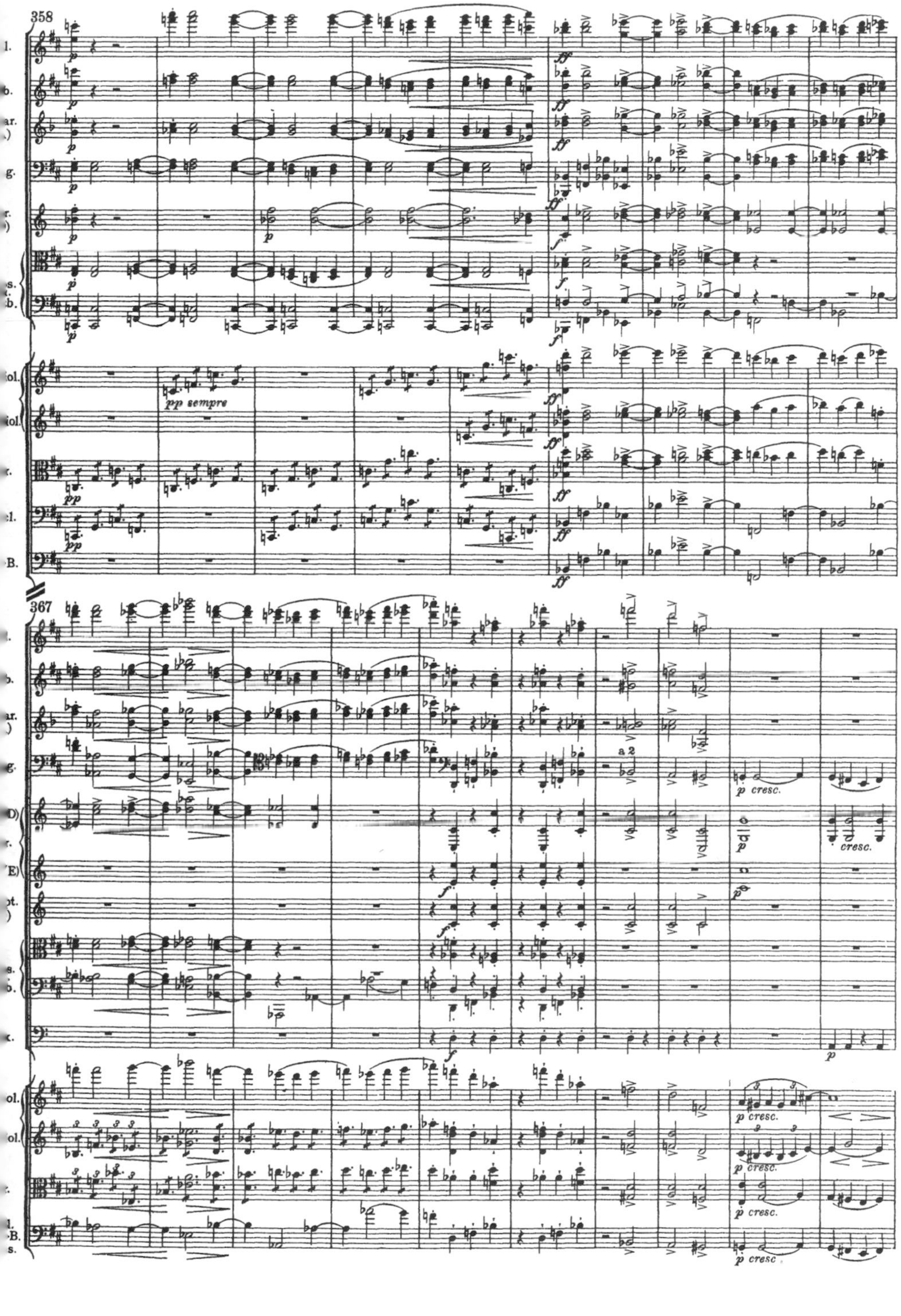
358
pp sempre
367
a 2
p cresc.
cresc.

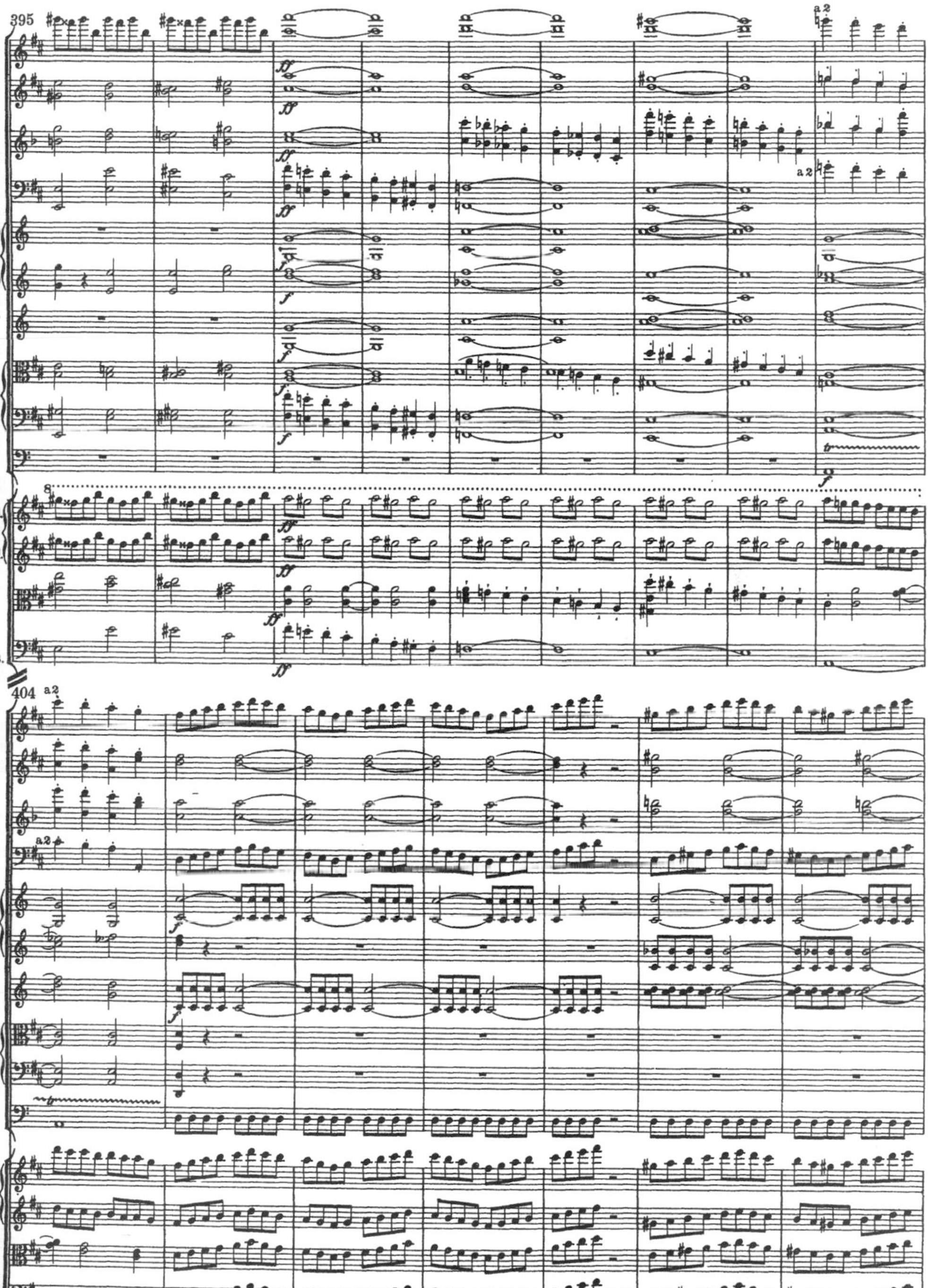
395
a 2
ff
f
8
404
a 2